Understanding Disabilities

UNDERSTANDING AUTISM

JESSICA RUSICK

Big Buddy Books

An Imprint of Abdo Publishing
abdobooks.com

abdobooks.com

Published by Abdo Publishing, a division of ABDO, PO Box 398166, Minneapolis, Minnesota 55439. Copyright © 2022 by Abdo Consulting Group, Inc. International copyrights reserved in all countries. No part of this book may be reproduced in any form without written permission from the publisher. Big Buddy Books™ is a trademark and logo of Abdo Publishing.

Printed in the United States of America, North Mankato, Minnesota.
052021
092021

THIS BOOK CONTAINS RECYCLED MATERIALS

Design: Emily O'Malley, Mighty Media, Inc.
Production: Mighty Media, Inc.
Editor: Megan Borgert-Spaniol
Content Consultant: Brenda Blackmore, Special Education Director
Cover Photographs: Shutterstock Images
Interior Photographs: Shutterstock Images, pp. 4, 5, 6, 8, 9, 10, 11, 12, 13, 14, 15, 16, 17, 18, 19, 20, 22, 23, 24, 25, 27, 28, 29; urbazon/iStockphoto, p. 7; vejaa/iStockphoto, p. 21

Library of Congress Control Number: 2020949913

Publisher's Cataloging-in-Publication Data
Names: Rusick, Jessica, author.
Title: Understanding autism / by Jessica Rusick
Description: Minneapolis, Minnesota : Abdo Publishing, 2022 | Series: Understanding disabilities | Includes online resources and index.
Identifiers: ISBN 9781532195723 (lib. bdg.) | ISBN 9781098216450 (ebook)
Subjects: LCSH: Autism--Juvenile literature. | Autism spectrum disorders--Juvenile literature. | Autistic people--Juvenile literature. | Autism--Diagnosis--Juvenile literature. | Autism in children--Treatment--Juvenile literature. | Social acceptance--Juvenile literature.
Classification: DDC 616.8982--dc23

CONTENTS

Talking at Recess 4
What Is Autism? 6
Autism Symptoms 10
Who Has Autism? 14
Autism at School 16
Social Skills 18
Being a Friend 22
Strengths 26
Golden Rules 28
Activities 29
Glossary 30
Online Resources 31
Index 32

Talking at Recess

Jaden loves dinosaurs. One day at recess, he tells his friend Ava about his favorite kinds. Jaden is so excited that he moves closer to Ava. Soon, he is in her personal space. Jaden doesn't realize this makes Ava uncomfortable.

Ava starts to say something. But Jaden continues to talk. This bothers Ava. However, Jaden doesn't realize Ava is upset. Jaden has trouble noticing how others are feeling. This is because Jaden has autism.

What Is Autism?

Autism is a **developmental** disability. It affects the way the brain works. People with autism can have trouble **communicating** and **behaving** with others.

It is important to accept and **appreciate** people's differences. You can show you accept and appreciate others by trying to learn about them. You might politely ask if they'll share how autism affects them.

Autism is different for everyone. Some autistic people have trouble talking to others. Others rarely speak at all.

Always use respectful language. This includes respecting how someone with autism chooses to **identify**. A classmate may call herself an autistic person. Or she may call herself a person with autism. Be sure to ask your classmate which language she prefers.

Remember

People with disabilities are not **victims**. This word makes it sound like having a disability is a bad thing. But a disability is not bad. It's just a difference!

"I am a person with autism."

Person First

Person-first language puts a person before his or her disability. People who use it believe people should not be defined by their disabilities.

"I am an autistic person."

Identity First

People who use **identity**-first language believe someone's disability is an important part of his or her identity. Many autistic people are proud to **identify** as such.

Autism Symptoms

Autism is also called autism **spectrum** disorder. Autism is a spectrum because it comes with a wide range of **symptoms**. Every autistic person is different. Some need more help than others to do everyday tasks.

Autism affects how people talk and act with others. Someone with autism may:

- ★ Have trouble understanding how others are feeling
- ★ Have trouble making his or her feelings known
- ★ Avoid looking others in the eyes
- ★ Have trouble keeping up a **conversation**
- ★ Not know when someone is joking or teasing
- ★ Not understand others' **body language** or the looks on their faces
- ★ Have trouble understanding simple questions

Autism can affect how people move. Someone with autism may:

- ★ **Repeat** movements such as rocking or hand-flapping
- ★ Have trouble with body movements and balance
- ★ Make faces or move in ways that don't match what he or she is saying

Autism can also affect **behavior**. Someone with autism may:

- ★ Become upset by changes to **routine**
- ★ Be easily affected by bright light, touch, and certain noises, clothing, or foods
- ★ Have a strong interest in a certain thing or subject
- ★ Talk about a favorite subject at length and not realize if the listener has lost interest
- ★ Not realize when he or she is in someone's personal space

Who Has Autism?

Autism is usually **diagnosed** at a young age. That's because doctors look for signs of it at regular checkups. Most kids are diagnosed between ages three and six. Autism continues into adulthood.

About 1 in 54 children in the United States has autism. Males are four times more likely than females to be diagnosed. However, doctors believe **symptoms** can be harder to recognize in females. Females may hide their symptoms more than males. So, many females with autism may not be diagnosed.

Males with autism are more likely to:
- ★ Separate from others in social settings
- ★ Lose control of their **emotions** in public
- ★ Display **repetitive behaviors**, such as lining up toys or other objects

Females with autism are more likely to:
- ★ Look and behave like other kids to fit in
- ★ Control their emotions when in public but then lose control at home
- ★ Display repetitive behaviors that are less noticeable, such as collecting dolls

Autism at School

School can be **challenging** for kids with autism. Areas such as hallways and lunchrooms are often noisy and bright. So, autistic kids may feel **overwhelmed**. Changes to **routine**, such as field trips, can also be overwhelming.

Certain tools and practices can help kids with autism do well in school. These include using ear plugs, sensory objects, and more.

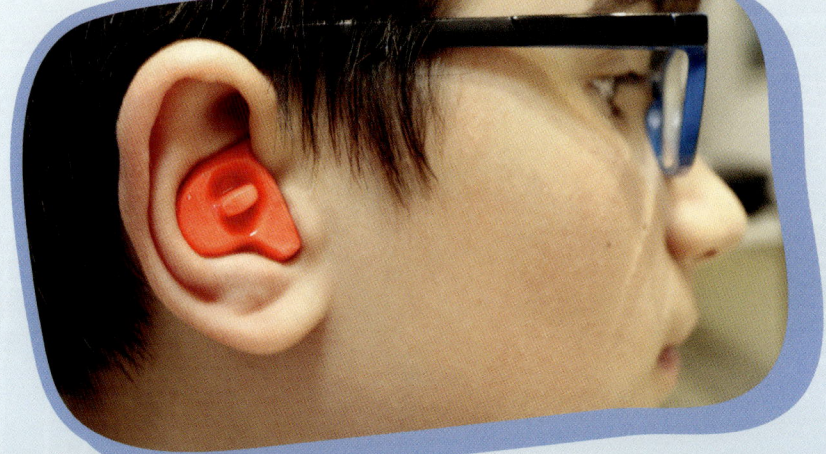

Autistic kids sometimes wear ear plugs to block out unwanted noise.

Autistic kids may keep their hands busy with squeeze balls, clay, and other sensory objects. This can help control repetitive movements.

Teachers help kids with autism prepare for expected changes in routine.

Kids with autism may take more breaks between tasks to avoid becoming overwhelmed.

Social Skills

Kids with autism often have trouble making friends. That's because many have trouble learning and using social skills. For example, an autistic person may not know how to start a **conversation** or join a game.

Kids with autism also have trouble noticing how others are feeling. For example, an autistic classmate may not realize you are sad. He may laugh instead of offering comfort.

Playing with others can take a lot of effort for autistic kids. Many find it easier to play alone.

Autistic kids may also **behave** in ways that others don't understand. For example, someone with autism may feel **overwhelmed** by crowds of people. When overwhelmed, kids with autism may cry, scream, or **repeat** movements. Autistic kids are more likely to be teased or bullied because of these behaviors.

Most people block out everyday sounds. But autistic people can find these sounds distracting and even upsetting.

Being a Friend

Everyone has his or her own strengths and **challenges**. That's okay! No matter what, everyone should be treated with respect.

There are many ways to be a good friend to an autistic person. It may take longer for your friend to answer a question or share his thoughts. Be kind and **repeat** yourself if needed.

Also remember to be understanding. Your friend may need to take breaks sometimes. This can happen when certain sounds, smells, or other senses become **overwhelming**. Give your friend space to calm down if he needs it.

Autistic kids may have trouble being social. But friendship is just as important to them as it is to anyone else.

More Ways to Be a Friend

Include Everyone
Invite your friend to play and explain how she can take part.

Stand Up to Bullying
Tell an adult if someone is being mean to your friend or classmate.

Communicate with Care

Some autistic kids **communicate** using pictures, sounds, or pointing. Use the method that your friend is most comfortable with.

Politely Speak Up

If your friend said something unkind, he may not realize it. So, nicely speak up if your feelings are hurt.

Strengths

Having autism can be **challenging**. However, many people say their autism helps them learn facts quickly and remember them well. Many also have the ability to **focus** for long periods on subjects that interest them. Autistic people have become successful actors, writers, and more.

Greta Thunberg

Greta Thunberg is a young **activist**. In 2018, she started a movement to stop **climate change**. Thunberg is autistic. She is proud that this makes her different from others. Thunberg says that "being different is a superpower."

Greta Thunberg was named Person of the Year by *Time* magazine in 2019. At 16 years old, she was the youngest person yet to receive this honor.

Golden Rules

Millions of people have disabilities. If you know someone with a disability, there may be times when you feel unsure of what to say or do. When in doubt, remember to treat others how you'd want to be treated. And, keep in mind these other golden rules:

- ★ Accept and respect differences
- ★ Use respectful language
- ★ Be kind and caring

Activities

Do you have any friends who have autism?
Invite them to join you for a fun activity.

Play a computer or video game

Put together a jigsaw puzzle

Play a board game

GLOSSARY

activist—a person who fights for a cause.

appreciate—to value or admire greatly.

behave—to act in a certain way. Behavior is the way a person acts.

body language—the movements or positions of the body that help show a person's feelings.

challenging (CHA-luhn-djing)—testing one's strengths or abilities. Something that is challenging is a challenge.

climate change—long-lasting change in Earth's weather and temperature patterns.

communicate (kuh-MYOO-nuh-kayt)—to share knowledge, thoughts, or feelings.

conversation—a talk between two or more people.

developmental—relating to the steps of natural growth.

diagnose (die-ugh-NOES)—to recognize something, such as a disability, by signs, symptoms, or tests.

emotion (ih-MOH-shuhn)—a state of mind or feeling.

focus (FOH-kuhs)—to give full attention to a task.

identify—to say or show who someone is.

identity—the set of features and beliefs that make a person who she or he is.

overwhelm—to strongly affect one's thoughts and feelings in a way that is too much to deal with.

repeat—to do or say something again. Something that repeats is repetitive.

routine (roo-TEEN)—a group of actions that are done regularly.

spectrum—a range of different kinds or types.

symptom—a noticeable change in the normal working of the body or mind.

victim—someone who has been harmed by an unpleasant event.

ONLINE RESOURCES

To learn more about autism, please visit abdobooklinks.com or scan this QR code. These links are routinely monitored and updated to provide the most current information available.

INDEX

acceptance, 6, 28
activities, 29

behavior, 4, 6, 11, 13, 15, 18, 19, 20, 25
being a friend, 22, 23, 24, 25, 28, 29
being respectful, 8, 22, 28

communicating, 6, 7, 11, 18, 25

diagnosing, 14

helpful tools and practices, 16, 17

identity, 8, 9

movements, 12, 17, 20

school, 4, 8, 16, 17, 18, 24
social skills, 4, 11, 13, 15, 18, 19, 23
spectrum, 10
strengths, 22, 26
symptoms, 7, 10, 11, 12, 13, 14, 15

teasing and bullying, 20, 24
Thunberg, Greta, 26, 27

United States, 14